THE BANDANNA BOOK

BY TY JUAN AHN

APPLESEED PRESS
KENNEBUNKPORT, MAINE

13 Digit ISBN: 978-1-60464-004-5
10 Digit ISBN: 1-60464-004-9

This book may be ordered by mail from the publisher. Please include $2.75 for postage and handling. Please support your local bookseller first!

Books published by Appleseed Press Gift Books are available at special discounts for bulk purchases in the United States by corporations, institutions, and other organizations. For more information, please contact the publisher.

Appleseed Press Gift Books
12 Port Farm Road
Kennebunkport, Maine 04046

Visit us on the web!
www.cidermillpress.com

Concept Creator: Toby Schmidt
Design by Jessica Disbrow Talley
Printed in China

1 2 3 4 5 6 7 8 9 0
First Edition

TABLE OF CONTENTS

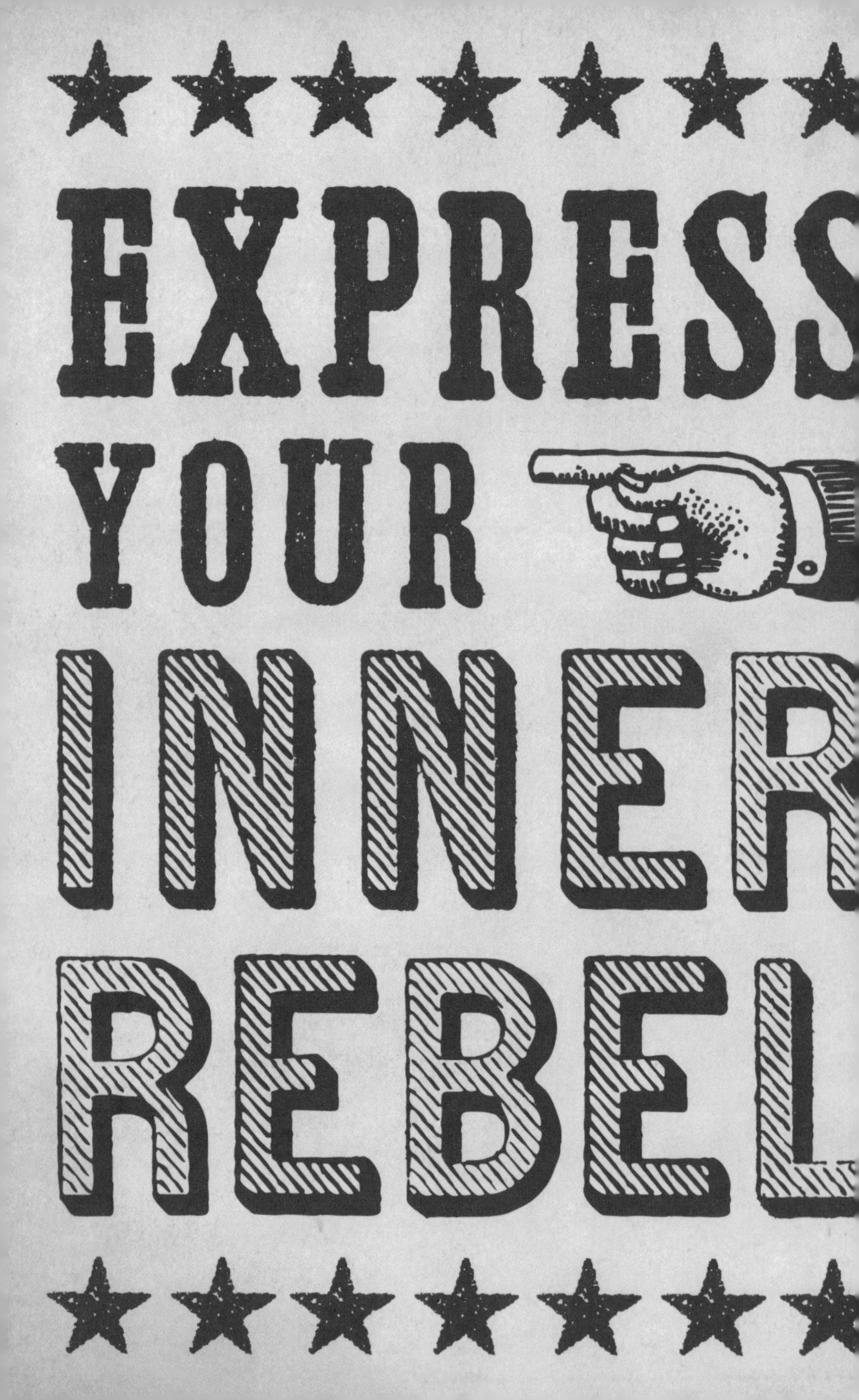
EXPRESS
YOUR
INNER
REBEL

CHAPTER 1

THIS BOOK IS NOT JUST ABOUT BANDANNAS,

it is really about you and about furthering your self-expression. The bandanna has a true cult following–wearing one says "individuality." Even if you are in a stadium full of bandanna-wearing bikers, you will stand out as unique and apart from the pack precisely because you are wearing a bandanna. Wrapping it around your head to cover your bald spot or shoving it in the breast pocket of your silk suit tells the world that you dare to be different. In and of itself, as a fashion statement, there is no other as versatile and widely accepted piece of gender-neutral clothing that has been worn by so many and says so much about the wearer. While it is much imitated, it has never truly been replaced, and many have tried–the kerchief, hanky, snot rag, do rag, scarf, and even burqa have not quite reached the level of popularity as the bandanna. And as you'll also find in this book, it's a darned handy thing to own.

WRAP
THIS
AROUND YOUR
THROAT

CHAPTER 2

From nooses to neckties, men and the women who love or hate them – or both – have been tying things around their necks since the beginning of time. Given how long ago the beginning of time was and all the fashion trends that have come and gone, the bandanna is relatively new to the fashion scene. And if anthropologists are correct about when primitive man first appeared on this planet, that means leafing through about seven million years of back issues of *Vogue* magazine. Thankfully for us, early primitive man limited his accessorizing to crudely carved clubs, and there was little concern over neckwear.

There are socio-historians who contend that neckwear can find its roots buried in the tribal doings of our hairy ancestors. Of course this isn't proven, but some suggest that prehistoric humans, not unlike apes, had to puff up and pound their chests to gain some respect and exert their authority. It could be that the rank of the top male often depended on how well he was able to exhibit his prowess with this infernal chest beating.

Based on this, one could then logically make the assumption that the need to have something adorn the neck, which brings attention to the chest–the center of power–is directly tied to man's primal lust for control and the need to dominate. While much of this is conjecture, there could be some credibility to the theory, because one glance into the archives of popular American television finds some pretty compelling evidence. After all, Fred Flintstone wore a tie.

DID YOU KNOW?
Some speculate that banditó comes from the word bandanna, since bandits often wore them as masks to conceal their identities.
OLÉ

★ ★

THE BIRTH OF NECKWEAR

ALL OF THAT HEADY TALK ASIDE, the earliest form of recorded neckwear appears in ancient Rome. History tells us that it was the fashion of Roman public speakers – read, statesmen – to wear neck cloths to protect their throats, keeping them warm so that they could pontificate for hours on end. Thankfully, today's politicians have abandoned that fashion trend, therefore exposing their throats to the cold and elements, and hopefully rendering them speechless (or strangled) by today's neckties. Roman soldiers also adopted neck cloths, as did soldiers from ancient China, to add some much-needed padding before they put on their armor. In all these cases, neck clothes were worn not for show but for function. The need for functionality drove the minimal neckwear use in the Middle Ages. It might have been the superstition that bodily ills entered one through the throat that had something to do with the continued popularity of a protective neckcloth, or perhaps soldiers felt more secure having their

★ ★

DID YOU KNOW?

As most know, the bandanna has morphed into significant fashion wear for gangs, most of whom consider it the flag of their gang nation. Color depicts which gang you belong to, and if you happen to wander into gang territory innocently wearing a bandanna and don't happen to be a member of any gang, much less the gang you ran into, you are in a heap of trouble. Not very comforting for those of us with babushka-wearing Bosnian grandmothers living in East L.A.

neck covered in battle. Or maybe they were just cold. It wasn't until the mid-1600s that the fashion scene embraced the idea of neckwear as a must-have accessory for men, thanks to the reign of the infamous dandy Louis XIV of France -- who also ushered in the mad male craze of wearing colorful tights, voluminous lace collars and flamboyant tower wigs. Legend has it that a regiment of crack Croatian mercenaries, who were celebrating their victory over the Turks, visited France and were presented as heroes to King Louis. The vain king,

★ ★ ★ ★ ★ ★ ★ ★ ★ ★ ★ ★ ★ ★ ★ ★ ★ ★ ★ ★

known for his compulsion for fashion, noticed that the officers wore brightly colored silk handkerchiefs around their necks. The king was so enthralled with these that he made them a royal insignia and created his own regiment of Royal Cravat. (The French word *cravat* comes from the Croatian, "kravate.") Thanks to high-profile people wearing them, cravats became standard issue. English gentlemen always wore some type of cloth around their necks, and the more elegant the better. Cravats were fashioned from plaid, embroidered linen, and other fabrics. They were often decorated with ribbon bows, lace, and tasseled string. Some were so high that a man couldn't turn his head, while others were thick enough to stop a sword thrust, which came in pretty handy during a duel.

DID YOU KNOW?

Bandannas were a fashion must for the four most famous cartoon turtles of the 1980s. Can you name the color of the bandannas that each of the Teenage Mutant Ninja Turtles wore? Better yet, can you even name them?

Leonardo - blue **Raphael - red**

Michaelangelo - orange **Donatello - purple**

PERHAPS NO FASHIONISTA is more closely tied to neckwear than the Englishman Beau Brummel, the veritable father of modern neckties and maybe very distant, second grand uncle-once-removed to the bandanna. Born George Bryan Brummell and not of royal or privileged birth, Brummell was able, through hearty pandering, to rise in the ranks of England's elite and make his mark on, of all places, their wardrobe. He focused on the cravat – developing complex and elaborate knots for varying social events and times of day, and catapulting this bit of fabric to a fashion statement in and of itself. By the late

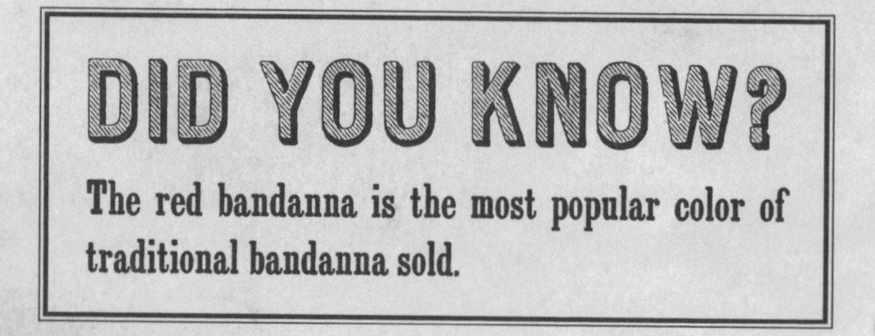

The red bandanna is the most popular color of traditional bandanna sold.

★ ★

1800s, there were over 32 ways to fashionably knot a cravat. As all super models know, when fashion is this important, it cannot be stopped. The cravat spread across the modern world of the 17th century and across the Atlantic Ocean to the colonists in America. The colonists eventually rebelled against all things English and chose to abandon the cravat for the simple bow tie and, eventually, the necktie. In search of their own independence but never having the guts to actually create something of their own, they stumbled upon a fashion that they could steal – the bandanna. In truth, the bandanna was not born from the inbreeding of the cravat and a woman's hanky. No, it actually

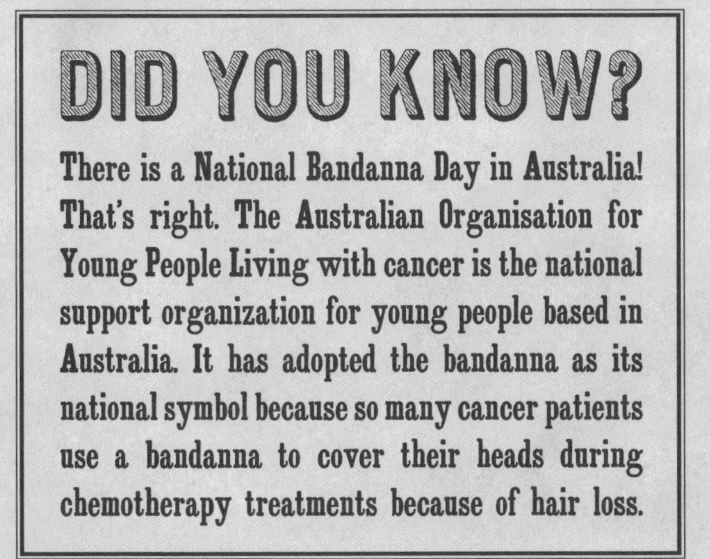

DID YOU KNOW?

There is a National Bandanna Day in Australia! That's right. The Australian Organisation for Young People Living with cancer is the national support organization for young people based in Australia. It has adopted the bandanna as its national symbol because so many cancer patients use a bandanna to cover their heads during chemotherapy treatments because of hair loss.

★ ★

FUN TO WEAR – AND SO MANY USES

THE BANDANNA WAS EASILY ADAPTABLE, something Americans loved and therefore developed all sorts of uses for. In the early days, these simple squares were used as handkerchiefs and neckerchiefs, head wraps, and bundle wraps. They were made of many fabrics in many patterns and colors and were imported not only from India but also from China, England, and Europe. The bandanna migrated onto the wide open spaces of the wild, wild west, where it became practically indispensable, and where its place as part of American history was permanently sealed. Initially, the bandanna was pulled up over the mouth to keep dust off the face and out of the mouths of the rough and ready. From there it took on a life of its own with the pioneers and their new lifestyle, becoming part of the true fabric of the land and morphing into many uses where the deer and antelope played. Banditos picked up on this fashion trend, realizing that if half the face–the recognizable half–is covered, the bandanna could

★ ★

be used as a mask, ultimately padding their own wallets. Red or blue bandannas were the original colors of choice. Today, bandannas have become the staple of any self-respecting school boy dressing up as a cowpoke for Halloween. But what young and old man alike doesn't dream of riding the range and living the western lifestyle? And while many youngsters only get to dress up as cowboys, for plenty of folks the cowboy tradition–and attire that includes a bandanna – is a way of life. For them, the bandanna still keeps out the dust and dirt while not only looking good, but providing a simple yet essential piece of fabric for doing all kinds of things like the ones in this book (and many more yet to be invented).

DID YOU KNOW?

Bandanna is also a language. It has morphed into a type of code, known as hanky code, which is used primarily in the gay community to indicate particular sexual references. Where the bandanna is worn, either in the right or left pocket, and its color can be translated to have varying meaning. The problem is, not everyone understands the code, which can cause a lot of confusion.

50
USES
From the obvious to the sublime
the bandanna has seen and done it al

CHAPTER 3

SLAVE TO FASHION

ACCESSORIES AND DOO DADS FOR YOUR DO RAG. FROM HEAD GEAR TO NECK WEAR

★ ★

1.

TRADITIONALIST

Wear the bandanna for its original intent—as a sassy neck accessory. Tie it around your neck, wear the knot in back for that early cowpoke look. Slide the knot in front if you're aching to look like a gondolier. Or slip it off to the side if you can't make up your mind.

* * * * * * * * * * * * * * * * * * * *

2. the FAUX APACHE

If tie dye is still a big part of your wardrobe and peace signs never grew old, then this look is for you. Fold the bandanna in one-inch increments, and tie it around your forehead, knot in back, over your hair. Try not to wash your hair for several days to capture the true Willie Nelson in you.

★ ★

3.

DRESS IT UP

Carefully folded, the bandanna can do as much if not more than the hanky when it comes to men's fashion. Nothing says sophisticate like a pocket square. Whether it be the presidential fold (folding the bandanna at right angles to fit in the pocket), or the TV fold (which looks similar but is folded diagonally with the point inside the pocket), the bandanna adds that bit of avant garde to any suit and occasion.

4.

If Junior wets through his diaper and there is no store in sight, rest assured. Having a spare bandanna can save the day. Just fold the fabric diagonally, slide it under baby's bottom, and bring the middle piece through baby's legs, knotting the remaining two ends in front and around the third piece. Happy, dry, and stylin'.

Nothing says down-home more than using your bandanna to fix those unsightly thin spots on the butt or knees of your worn-out jeans. If you use them copiously, you will have a pair that is all bandanna, kept together by bits and pieces of jean.

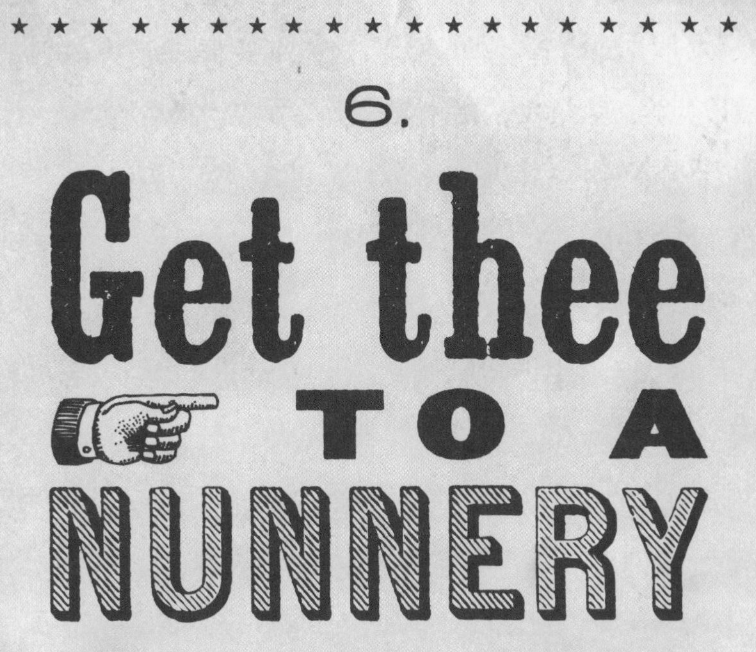

In a pinch, the bandana also doubles as a handy veil, for those devout in faith, who want to keep the crowns of their heads covered out of respect. Just toss it on your head as is and start praying.

★ ★

7. & 8.

THIGH HIGH

There was a time when wearing a bandanna on your thigh spelled 'c-o-o-l.' Reliving the Chachi "Happy Days" era might be fun, if not offbeat. Or was that Punky Brewster? Just pick a thigh, any thigh, and tie one on.

CHEST ENHANCER

Tired of your front looking like your back? When scrunched up, the bandanna can add two cup sizes to your frame. A perfect C cup.

★ ★

9. HOBO HANDBAG

Lest we forget, the bandanna was the original suitcase for bums bumming a ride on the rails, once called a bindle-stick for those word purists. Revive this traditional way of travel by selecting a slim and refined old branch, about three feet long. Stuff all your worldly belongings into a laid out bandanna, and then tie the edges securely at the far end. Toss it over your shoulder, smear some coal dust on your face, and get on the busy end of your thumb.

How do you protect your neck from the damaging rays of the sun? Ouch. You open your bandanna, place it on your head, with most of the cloth hanging over the back of your neck, and stick a ball cap on. Works like a charm. And folks might think you're a sheik.

★ ★

11.

TO BELT OR NOT TO BELT

Depending on your girth, more than one bandanna might do the trick. Just tie the ends in knots and slide it through your loops. Or wear it like a sassy sash on your hips, or the side of your head if you're from East LA.

Tying a bandanna on your car's antenna, providing you have a car that has one, says you are hippy friendly. Or, if it breaks down, it indicates that you are in distress. Or make it a snap to find your car in a crowded lot. No antenna? Try your side view mirror, your tailpipe or your fender.

★ ★

13.

STEER CLEAR

A red bandanna makes the perfect warning for drivers behind you when you are carrying long, wooden 2' by 4's. Tie it on the end to make sure you don't decapitate the guy behind you with a sudden stop.

* *

14. & 15.

DIP STICK CLEANER

Time to check the oil? Why wipe the murky mess on your sleeve or your lips? Your multiple-use bandanna can do the trick.

HOT SEAT PREVENTER

Why spend money on one of those ungainly window shades for your windshield? A bandanna snugly tucked into each bucket seat is much handier - not to mention, a smart look.

16.

Got a leaky radiator?

This is better than a mechanic. Just stop the leak with a bandanna and get to your nearest repair shop.

17. BETTER THAN A HANDY WIPE

A bandanna is perfect for the incidental messes any driver has to deal with, whether it be dealing with wiping off bird poop, mopping up fast-food spills, getting the steam off a windshield after a few hours of smooching your best girl. It's an all-purpose cleaning cloth. And will never tell your secrets.

18. CAR MAT COVERS

Just shampooed your car carpets? Don't let your friends spill latte all over them. Place your bandannas on the mats, snugly fit around the edges, until the shampoo dries. Then tell your friends to walk home.

★ ★ ★ ★ ★ ★ ★ ★ ★ ★ ★ ★ ★ ★ ★ ★ ★ ★ ★ ★

19.

Steering WHEEL COVER

Forget lamb's wool. Try bandannas to cover your steering wheel. This will take two, but wrap them around the wheel, and use a shoelace, plastic twist ties or thin leather straps to keep them in place. This should take you about six hours to do.

Keeping in line with good driver-ship, tying a bandanna to the back of your hitch notifies other motorists of the possibly deadly metal object sticking out of the back your vehicle which threatens to rip open the undercarriage of theirs if they are tailgating.

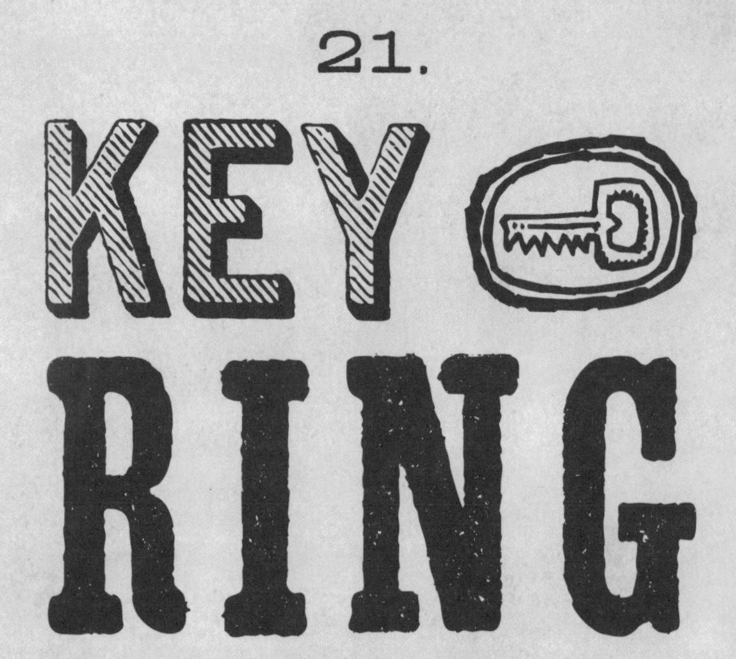

Tie your keys to your wrist with your bandanna, especially if you're prone to misplacing them or dropping them accidentally down an open sewer.

There isn't a picture frame around that couldn't stand to have a bandanna make-over. All it takes is glue and patience. Place the picture frame on the reverse side of the bandanna. Cut a hole in the middle with enough fabric to pull through to the other side. Cut slits on the diagonal. Glue them to the opposite side of the frame. Pull the remaining fabric around the edges, trim fabric and glue in place.

★ ★

23.

Lid covers

Tired of all those boring jars of pickled beets with those tinny looking covers? Ugh. Take a bandanna, cut it into eight squares, secure them on each cover with a rubber band, and place them back in your cupboard. Or better yet, display them on your window sill for guests to oooh and ahhhh over. For even more fun, cover any ugly jar in your fridge or cupboard by reversing the process. Show your canning pride.

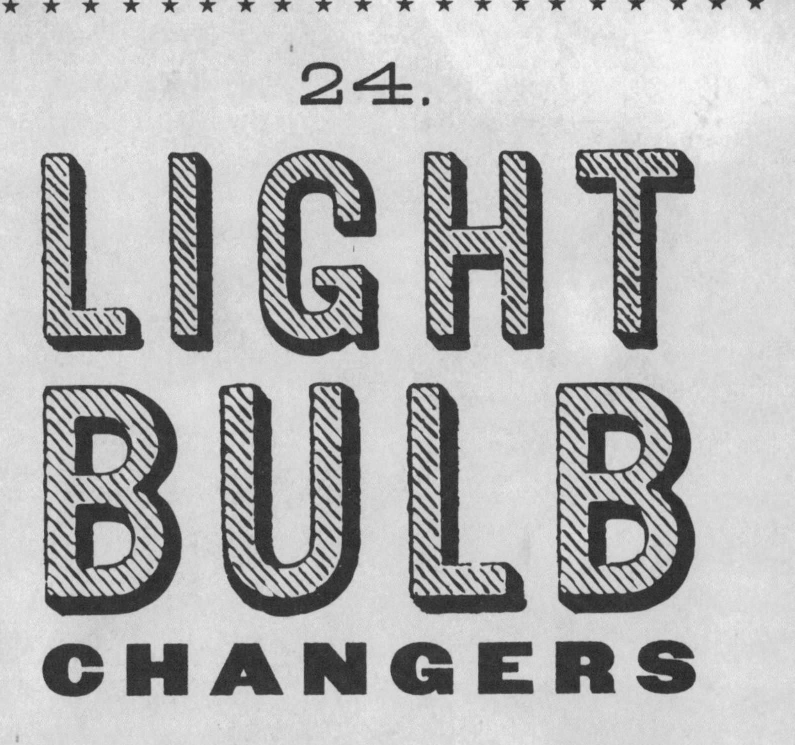

The days of singeing your fingertips are over. A bandanna bunched up in your hand has amazing grippage. It can also be used to pry open stubborn jar lids and as a dusting rag in a pinch.

25. Wine bottle APRON

What's better than wrapping a linen napkin around your 1787 Chateau Lafite when you serve it? (Probably not serving it all.) But if you have to, why not indulge your wild side and wrap a bandanna around it instead. After all, expensive wine speaks for itself. But you can add the outerwear.

26. Gardener's KNEE PADS

Knees on your pants crusted with mud? Well, put away the stain remover. Just tie a bandanna around each knee, and go jump into the soil.

27.

ITCH THIS

Sensitive to poison ivy?

Well, you don't have to touch it ever again, or ruin a pair of expensive garden gloves by pulling out the unwanted weeds. Wrap a bandanna around your hand, and knot it at the wrist. After you manhandle the itchy weed and show it who's boss, throw the bandanna away to prevent spreading.

28. LUGGAGE TAG

Who doesn't have problems identifying their black-wheeled luggage at the airport? Not you. Tie a bandanna securely around the handle and just wait at the carousel for yours to appear. You might even start a trend.

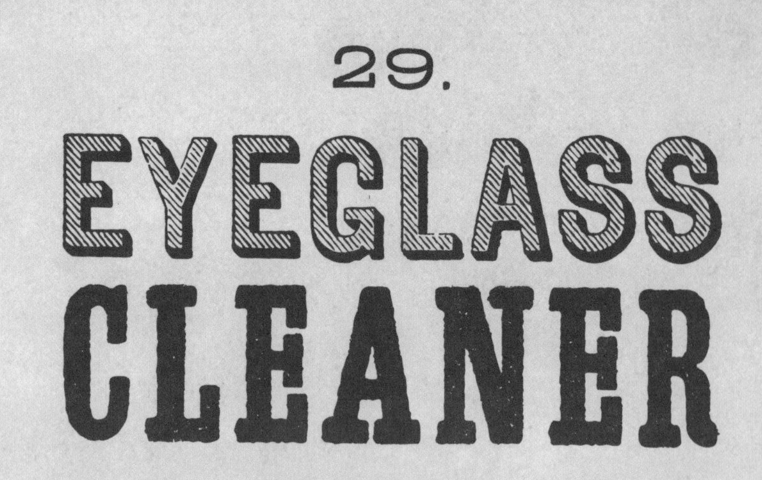

Nothing is quite as soft as a well-worn bandanna. So soft in fact that it can be used to get the schmootz off your sensitive eyeglasses without concern of scratching or marring the lenses.

* *

30.

Forget the cheese cloth. Try wetting a fresh bandanna and letting the fabric act as a natural method to separate out the egg whites for that perfect meringue. Or use it to filter out unfiltered water. Leave the rust in the bandanna and use it for your next hobo trip.

31.

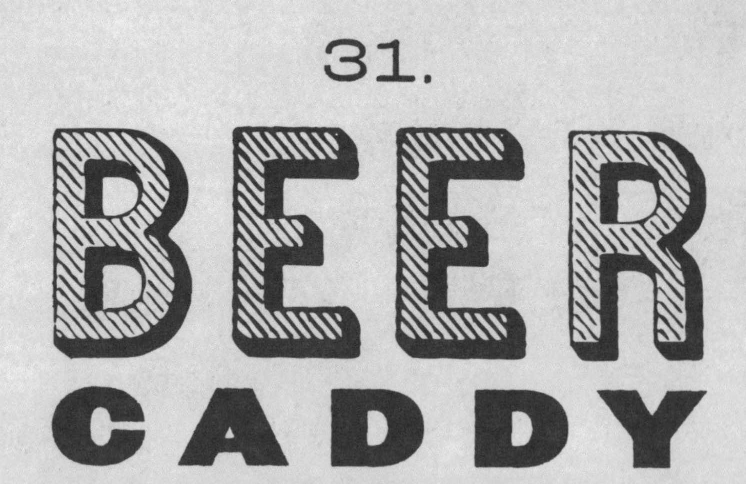

Not enough room in the fridge for your booze? Pack your bandanna with small ice slivers and a six of beer, knot the end, leaving an opening big enough to pull out a can or two, and hang it on the doorknob to the garage door.

32.

Don't worry about finding a shoe tree for all your fine leather shoes. Just stuff your bandannas inside the toes, secure in the knowledge that they will fit next time you wear them.

★ ★ ★ ★ ★ ★ ★ ★ ★ ★ ★ ★ ★ ★ ★ ★ ★ ★ ★ ★

33.

POTPOURRI HOLDER

Take your bandanna and stuff it with some sweet-smelling lavender, Queen Anne's lace, coffee grounds and old wrestler's socks. Use it in drawers or closets to add fragrance to your life.

And he loves cat nip. So have a ball driving him crazy with a bandanna ball stuffed with his favorite addictive herb.

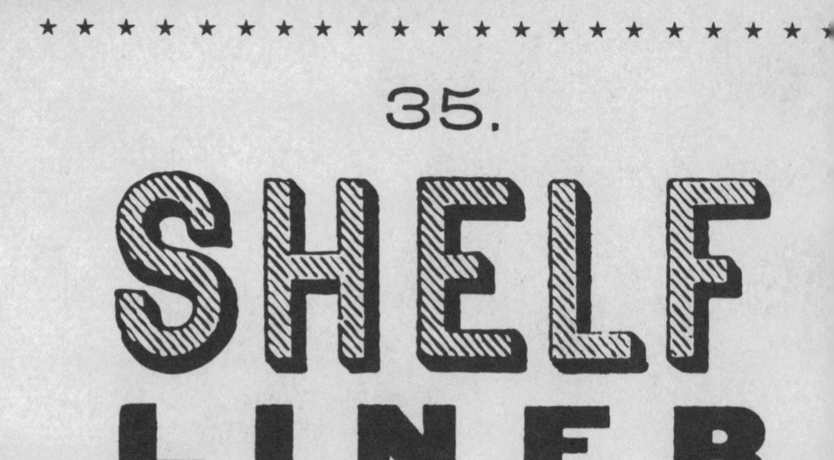

Boring best describes the shelf liners on the market today. Spiff up your kitchen design by adding calico to your shelves. This even works in the refrigerator and acts as a nifty spill collector.

★ ★

36.

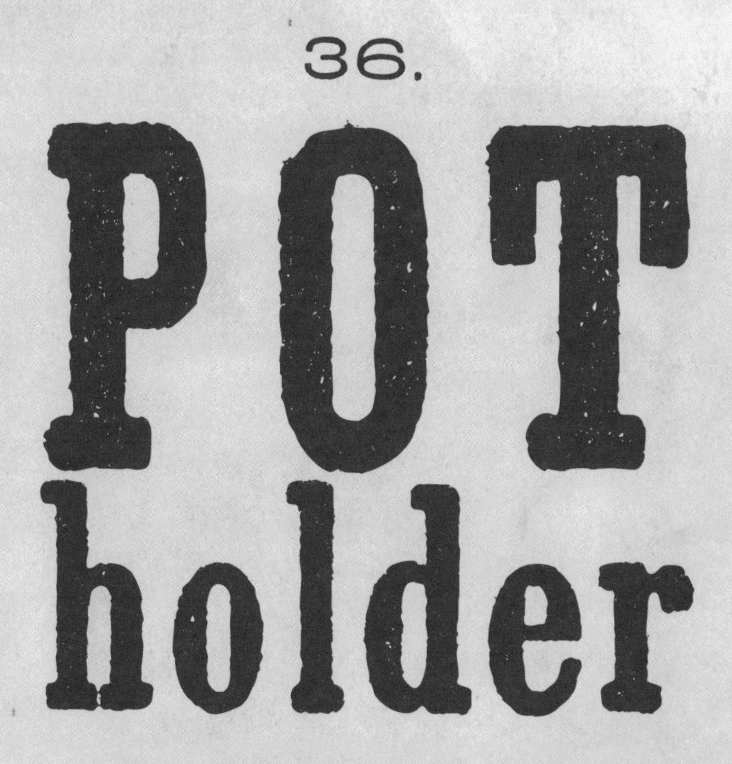

In a pinch, don't use your sleeve or the wet dish towel (ouch) to pull a steaming hot casserole out of the oven. Grab your bandannas, would you?

Any new mommy knows the trick of dimming the lampshade with a scarf. Well, what about draping a bandanna? Let the kid know his roots early on.

Appeal to your inner germ-a-phobe.

Use the bandanna to pick up the telephone, cover the toilet seat in a public place, or reach for a door handle. Never come in contact with another germ again. Even wear one when you shake hands.

★ ★

39. & 40.

Shoe polisher

With a little spit, your bandanna rivals the best shoe polish in town.

Fits the bill for someone who has everything, someone who has nothing, or someone who just needs a bandanna.

* *

41. & 42.

STAND OUT IN A CROWD

Meeting friends at the theatre, flagging down a taxi or just desperate for attention, try tying a brightly colored bandanna on a stick and waving it. Believe it or not, crowds will indeed gather.

Pack your lunch

Why invest in a lunch pack? Use a bandanna to handily wrap your baguette and goat cheese for work. When you're all done, you can wipe the crumbs off your face with it.

43. MOVIE THEATER SEAT SAVER

In your desperate rush to find the best seat in the house, you bypass the popcorn stand. Leave your bandanna royally displayed, and you can head back to gather up your bucket of heart clogging, palm-oil infused popcorn, loaded with faux butter and salt.

★ ★

44. Making a BALD MAN COOL

The bandanna should be singlehandedly credited for adding a bit of couture to those whose scalps are lacking. What bald man hasn't donned a bandanna, knotted smartly in the back, to protect his thinning or exposed pate from the sun. If this doesn't say 'look at me,' what does?

★ ★

45.

BANNER waving

Carrying a spare bandanna, especially if you are an athlete, comes in handy when you want to rub it in the face of your opponent. If you win, you can run around waving your bandanna like an obnoxious person. If you lose, you can use it for weeping profusely.

46.

Let the gentleman in you shine. Lay your freshly pressed bandanna over the nearest puddle and let your damsel saunter across, keeping her shoes dry and feet fresh.

★ ★

47. & 48.

TORTURE USES

A bandanna, with the very tip dipped in ice water, makes a mean rat tail, with just the right amount of snap. Twisted into a rope, it can act as a pair of handcuffs, or a garrotte. Note: Please do not try this at home. We are professionals.

WEAPON FOR BIBLICAL FIGHTS

On the off chance you might be coming up on Goliath any day soon, keep a bandanna at the ready, with a supply of rocks. Just in case.

★ ★ ★ ★ ★ ★ ★ ★ ★ ★ ★ ★ ★ ★ ★ ★ ★ ★ ★ ★

49.

Make a bandanna map

Draw where you are going on your bandanna, which you can then keep as a keepsake. You can also draw lots of attention when staring blankly at it in St. Peter's square. Look at it this way – you are never lost with a map around your neck.

★ ★

50. Survival OF THE MOST COLORFUL

Bandannas have been the constant companion of outdoorsmen for years. Use them to mark a trail, wipe the sweat from the brow, wet in a stream for instant relief, wrap around the arm for snake bite venom removal, spray one with repellent and let it hang from your belt, as a bear bag when hiking, or as replacement toilet paper.

GO
AHEAD!
TIE
ONE ON

★ ★

ABOUT APPLESEED PRESS

Great ideas grow over time. From seed to harvest, Appleseed Press labors to bring fine reading and entertainment together between the covers of its creatively crafted books. Our grove bears fruit twice a year, publishing a new crop of titles each Spring and Fall.

VISIT US ON THE WEB AT

www.appleseedpress.com

OR WRITE TO US AT

12 Port Farm Road

Kennebunkport, Maine 04046